DAY BY DAY LIVING
with
EPILEPSY

DAY BY DAY LIVING
with
EPILEPSY

RALPH BROOKS

Copyright © Ralph Brooks.

All rights reserved. No part of this book may be reproduced in any form or by any electronic or mechanical means, including information storage and retrieval systems, without permission in writing from the publisher, except by reviewers, who may quote brief passages in a review.

ISBN: 978-1-64921-232-0 (Paperback Edition)
ISBN: 978-1-64921-233-7 (Hardcover Edition)
ISBN: 978-1-64921-231-3 (E-book Edition)

Some characters and events in this book are fictitious. Any similarity to real persons, living or dead, is coincidental and not intended by the author.

Book Ordering Information

Phone Number: 347-901-4929 or 347-901-4920
Email: info@globalsummithouse.com
Global Summit House
www.globalsummithouse.com

Printed in the United States of America

CONTENTS

Acknowledgement ix
Introduction xi

A Boy's Encounter With An Epileptic Seizure 1
A Young Man's Coming to Terms 3
My Girlfriend Let Me Go 7
Getting Fired 9
Seeing My Son Have A Seizure 11
A Positive Attitude 13
The Danger I Face Everyday 16
What Is Epilepsy? 19
Questions about Epilepsy 21
Epilepsy In The Workplace 26
Day by Day Living with Epilepsy 32
Living With Epilepsy 34

Poetry and Children's Poem CPPGS80-91

Day By Day 39
My Talk To My Son 40
Kids Stay In School 41
Always Give God The Glory 43
American Poet 44
Change 46
A Cloud Of Endless Rain 48
Not What I Do Most 50

Can We Chat?	52
True Friendship	54
Who Could It Be?	56
Your Dreams Are What Make You	57
Love Is	58
What Can I Say?	59
Memories	60
Very Nice To See	61
Childhood	62
First	63
How Long Has It Been	64
The Lord's Prayer	65
Meeting My Son's School Teacher	66
My Senior Year (Class of 1983)	67
A Shout Out To All The Rappers	69
A Penny On Head	72
The Magic In Your Eyes	74
Grandparents	76
Cold World	77
The Barber Shop	78
Coffee And Tea	79
As Long As I Live	81
My High School Girlfriend	82
Born In Alabama	83
911	85
Spanish Music	87
McDonald's	89
Merry-Go-Round	90
I Love To Swing	92
Rainbow	94
Putting Your Children To Bed	96
Time-Out	98
Giraffe	100

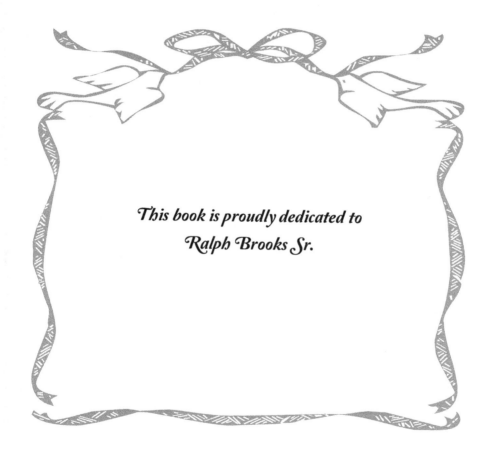

This book is proudly dedicated to Ralph Brooks Sr.

ACKNOWLEDGEMENT

I cannot express enough how thankful I am for the following individuals who have assisted me tremendously through the reprocessing of publishing Day by Day Living with Epilepsy: My publishing and marketing Consultant, Jerry Ryans, who helped me by recommending a professional publishing package along with Yvonne Johnson, my Check IN Coordinator, who designed the front and back covers of the book. To Darlene Greco, Mac Greco, Darrell Ingram and Gene Marshall, I will be forever grateful for your contribution and support in completing this project.

In addition, I want to give a special thank you to my senior editor, Sarjoo Devani, as he has been the guiding force behind the edification and proofreading of the book and I am eternally grateful for his guidance. Listed below is his email and website address in case you may need assistance with editing and proofreading:

Sarjoo@crazedandrephrased.global
WWW.crazedandrephrased.global

I also want to thank our GOD ALMIGHTY because without his grace and blessing this book would not have been possible.

In conclusion, I would like to acknowledge the belated, Zig Ziglar. My director, Cathy Magbee, took me to see him live in Orlando, Florida. Mr. Ziglar accompanied by his daughter on stage stated in a quote,

"You don't have to be great to start, but you have to start to be great".

Those sixteen words will live in my heart forever as a spark to never be afraid to start.

INTRODUCTION

What can I say about epilepsy? This is the question I often ask myself. My father died in his sleep at home from what doctor's say was a Generalized Tonic Clonic (grand mal seizure). When it happened I felt empty, and it inspired me to write a poem called "Day by Day," which explains the way I felt then and the way I feel now. Time has made me strong, and has given me a chance to heal.

My father's death motivated me to write this book because I have personally experienced the seizures and attacks similar to what he used to have. My family was not educated on what to do during these attacks, and we did what we thought was right at the time. Growing up with my father's illness was difficult for me because I felt helpless in not knowing what to do when he would have a seizure.

As a reader, I want you to take this journey with me, from my childhood days to my life as an adult dealing with epilepsy. When I was eight years old, I was diagnosed with having absence (petit mal seizures). Being so young, I didn't know what that meant. I was required to take medication that made me extremely sick. I felt different compared with rest of the kids and it was difficult watching the other children live healthy lives.

Each day is a struggle for me to live with epilepsy. Each person with epilepsy reacts differently during a seizure. I am dedicated to educating as many people as I possibly can about epilepsy. It is my hope this book will give a better understanding of seizures and how they can be controlled with the proper treatment regimen.

The workplace can be a challenging setting, placing co-workers in a dilemma if they are uneducated about the proper techniques for handling a person suffering from seizures. Speaking from experience, I learned that the best teacher is the person, who suffers from epilepsy, because I had to educate my friends and co-workers about how to handle my specific condition.

A BOY'S ENCOUNTER WITH AN EPILEPTIC SEIZURE

I can remember one day when I was 12 years old. My father and I were riding down the road in his car when, all of a sudden, I heard him cry out as he fell over and into my lap. The car crashed into a ditch, and with my young boy strength, I pulled my father out from the car to safety.

I grabbed my leather wallet out of my pocket and tried to put it in his mouth, because I had seen my mother and sister do this when he would have a seizure at home. They told me that this would stop him from biting his tongue.

His body felt stiff at first, and then his arms and legs began jerking uncontrollably. I tried to hold him down but I was not successful. This phase lasted for about 30 seconds before he started breathing normally again.

After the seizure, I asked him if he knew what had happened to him. My father was confused and acted as if nothing had transpired, then asked for the keys to the car. I explained to him what had occurred and told him to relax, and that I would take care of him. I was afraid of driving him home because he kept saying, "Stop the car and let me drive." I was also afraid that this could happen again, as he would have another seizure.

When I got to the house, I passed on what had occurred with my father. My mother praised me for how well I handled the situation. I felt more at ease when she asked if I had put something in my father's mouth.

The day my father had this attack, it really affected my life, because it was my first time being isolated with my father whilst he was having a seizure. I had never experienced this on my own. My family members had always been there when a seizure would take place, so to be alone with him was very frightening. Today, I know better, that one never puts anything in the mouth of a person having an epileptic seizure.

A YOUNG MAN'S COMING TO TERMS

My brother and I were at a Friday night football game and, just before half time, another incident took place. My friend collapsed in the middle of the field and went into a Generalized Tonic Clonic (grand mal seizure). Most of the people in the stands were amazed because they were not used to seeing this, but my brother and I had seen it before...

I could identify what was happening because I had seen my father have the same kind of seizure. Although, after seeing it happening again to my friend, I was still startled to be faced with this condition. I knew I had to acquire more information about it.

Fortunately for my friend, the paramedic crew was available at each game to assist him and perform first aid, or to provide any other help that was needed. When I would see my friend in school, I wanted to tell him that my father had the same type of attacks as he did, but I didn't.

My football career started the next year after my friend had graduated. In my junior year we won the state championship in football and made the playoffs in basketball and baseball. I played all three sports. My senior year, we were the area 6, region 3 champs and the 2A state runners-up.

During my senior year in the state championship game, I took a bad hit from a player on the other team in the last play of the game. As I walked off the field, my neck started hurting me bad, but I paid no attention to it, and as I got to the fence, I collapsed.

The next thing I perceived, I was in the hospital but didn't know the reason why. I had to undergo numerous medical tests, including MRI, EEG and CAT scans. I asked my doctor if I was going to die, and what to do to prepare at a young age in life. He said that I had a grand mal seizure, and that people seldom died from them, but that I needed to make sure I took my medication on a daily basis.

I had to stay in the hospital for about two months. I would beg the doctor everyday to let me go home but the answer was "no". I was not prepared for what would happen to me while I was under the doctor's care. At midnight the nurse would come and wake me up to give me a shot. When the morning came, breakfast would be served at 6am and my medication would be provided so that I could rest.

They would wake me up at 12 noon for lunch and to take blood to check my blood level to make sure that I stayed in the range between 12 and 15 on my Dilantin level(anti-seizure medication). This was very important because anything lower than that could cause me to have a seizure. I hated this time of day, as my arm was so sore from giving blood all the time, that it made me weak. My nurse was very nice and respectful but I felt uncomfortable because she had to give me a bath everyday.

I was a senior in high school with my whole future ahead of me. How could this be happening to me? My friends came to visit me in the beginning but most of them didn't own a car and depended on their parents to take them around.

When nighttime came, dinner was served and more blood was taken from my arm. There were no windows to stare out of, and only now my mother would come to visit me. I was placed into what they call a Florida Neck Brace, as it is supposed to support your neck. It was hard to wear, it stunk and itched all the time.

I had waited all my life to graduate from high school and be the first one in my family. I was in the hospital on the day of my graduation and my blood level was low, I begged the doctor to let me go to my graduation, and the nurse finally persuaded him to let me go.

When I got there and the door opened, you could hear a pin if someone dropped one. Everyone in the building was shocked and in disbelief to see a superstar all braced up and in a wheel chair. I will never forget this moment. Everyone in the building was standing on their feet and began to clap their hands.

I was so excited about being the first one in my family to graduate from high school that I forgot I was hurt. There were eight in my family and my three sisters, all older than me, dropped out of high school. My father had a third grade education and my mother only went to the ninth grade. I always wanted to be a football star but I also wanted to make history with being on stage to get my diploma.

When the nurse was rolling me down the hall, I moved her hands away and began to do it myself, that's how bad I wanted it. My inside was so fired up that I knew I was going to get sick again before the night was over. I made it to the stage and my friends had to wheel me up to where everyone else was sitting.

When they called my name I jumped up out of the wheelchair and walked to the podium. I didn't make it back to my seat since the excitement was so much that my heart couldn't take it, so I did what I do best, I collapsed on stage, but I had my diploma.

I couldn't believe that they were moving me to another hospital about an hour away from where my family lived. I thought I had it bad but this was cake to where I had to go. My new nurse was mean and didn't treat me with respect. She put me through some tough times with therapy and always never warned me when it was time to get a shot or take my blood.

I was told that I had to stay another two months and hopefully then I could go home. I knew I had to stay positive and keep praying that the Lord would see a way somehow to let me go home and be with my family and friends. After doing exactly two months the doctor finally said that I could go home.

I never hope that anyone has to spend as much time as I've had to spend in the hospital throughout my life. I can't think of a year from the time I was 18 years old up until now, that I haven't been in the hospital. I don't know how I have been able to keep some of my jobs because stress can cause you to have a seizure and I've had plenty of those.

MY GIRLFRIEND LET ME GO

When I started having seizures in high school it really changed my life. I can't say that I was in love when all I knew is that I had a girlfriend. Once I got hurt in football things for us changed like overnight. The things I used to say to her didn't matter anymore. We had our own little secret place we would go but now we couldn't go anymore. The poems I use to write were poems with no meaning to them now.

Then it happened one day, I was reading this book called a Day No Pigs Would Die. I was wondering how could someone title a book like that, and what is the meaning of that title. At the end of the book it said that the man who had butchered hogs for years had died, so no pigs would have to lose their lives that day.

My girlfriend at the time wrote me a letter and said: "Ralph I can't be your girl anymore." Apart of me died that day, but I thought about the book and the meaning of the story. Sometimes in life you have to lose a life to gain a life, so I met someone new. I was hurt, but I had made up my mind that I wouldn't move away to get away from all my friends who knew that we had broken up.

I never had the nerves to ask my mother about relationships and girls because back then I didn't feel comfortable talking about that. I just knew that I couldn't bring no babies home if I wanted to stay under the same roof with my other brothers and sisters.

I went to live with my cousin and got a job working in a sewing plant to get my mind off of everything. I felt like I needed a new start in life and try to make the best of what I had. My mother was always supportive of everything that I did and we always remained good friends.

I had to make new friends who were not always that easy to have, when you had epilepsy. The interesting thing is that people are surprised that you have it because we too are normal people just like everyone else. The worst thing is when it happens and people around you are not educated about seizures, then it can become something they don't want to be around. Still today, I am shocked that I have it.

GETTING FIRED

I have only been fired one time in my life from a job. I was working a nightshift from 6pm until 6am for three straight days and then I would be off for four days after that. My body was not used to my medication so it was hard for me to stay focused on anything and my mind would wonder a lot.

The night that I got fired my boss didn't want to let me go. I would go in the bathroom after eating lunch at 11pm, but I couldn't stay awake after that and would sleep for about four hours and not realize I was gone that long.

I had to learn how to take my medication so that my body would get on a timely routine. I was taking my medicine whenever I felt like taking it and it caused me problems for a long time. I now take it at the same time all the time and my results are much better than in the past.

I thought losing my girlfriend was bad, but nothing comparable to like losing a job. I took work very seriously because my mother worked two jobs and never complained about anything-she just kept going. I couldn't hold down one job and was scared to let her know that I didn't have a job.

At this point in my life what is next for me? When you think that you can see the light, you can't. My mother and father got divorced after 15 years of marriage, and now I had to go back home without a job. I finally had to let her know, and she got me a job with her as a cook.

My old girlfriend started talking to one of my good friends, but I told her she made her choice and I wished her the best. I had to get all of these thoughts out of my head and go on with life.

After losing my job, I felt like I let myself down. I had been down in life before and always bounced back, but this wasn't a rubber ball. I still found a way to get myself back on track.

SEEING MY SON HAVE A SEIZURE

The first time I had seen my son having a seizure was shocking. They called me from work and said that I needed to come home. When I got to the apartment complex, there was a nurse who lived there, and she was helping him. She gave him to me and I took him inside my apartment.

I asked his mother what had happened and she said they were riding in the car and she looked in the front mirror and saw him shaking in his car seat. She stopped the car and began to talk to him until he came out of the seizure. She knew not to put anything in his mouth and to turn him on his side, and put something soft under his head.

Then all of sudden as we were talking it happened again, he started to have a seizure. I knew in my heart that he would be all right but at the same time it was a weird feeling. His mother was terrified and began to cry, so I tried to comfort both of them at the same time.

I had to take a week off from work to make sure that he was okay. When I got ready to take him to the doctor it happened again. This time it was different because he knew something was going to happen, so he began to cry. The hardest part for me was watching my son lose his body unwillingly and not be able to do anything.

I learned that no matter how much you know about what to do when someone is having a seizure, when it's your own child and you're the parent, it's a different feeling. The reason I say this is because for the past two years I have been to a camp for kids who suffer with chronic illnesses. I worked as a counselor for one week without telling them that I have epilepsy. I am able to handle kids at camp with no problems, and manage to stay focused at all times.

When I see my son suffer with what my father and I have experienced it breaks my heart. A part of me wants to get inside his body and fight with him-but we have to find a cure for this chronic illness called epilepsy.

I always would think about how did my mother react when she would see me have a seizure. Watching my son having a seizure has helped me realize as a parent what my family experienced with me.

There so many things we can see in life, I hope that no mother or father has to see something like this happen to their children. I try not to take it for granted any time that is given to my son and me. Time is not something you sit back and watch go by, for me it is what I do with this time.

When I think about epilepsy, I have no hate for it. I just want to beat it in everything that I do in the future. People may not let you forget that you have it, but don't let them forget that you can do everything they do and sometimes even better.

My son and I are so much alike, we never give up and we keep pushing. We will never be measured by the way we stand from all of the places we have fallen. I will always be watching, learning and trying to help others as well as my son have a better chance at life.

One day I hope we can find a cure and help as many epileptic patients, as we can enjoy life one day at a time. I don't know what the future holds but until it comes I will always be shooting for the stars.

What a smile it would bring to my face that one day my son will be writing a book about his life and being a part of that is special. There is so much we have to live for and we must apply our talents and aim for greatness.

A POSITIVE ATTITUDE

The most important thing for me is to keep a positive attitude. When something can have complete control over your mind for 30 seconds or more it's hard to stay strong. I try to stay content no matter what situation I may be in. I try to counteract what is happening to me, and sometimes it works and sometimes it doesn't.

When I was a sophomore at Eufaula High School, in Eufaula, Alabama, I was not eligible to play football. I moved from a town called Jackson Gap, Alabama to live with Bertha Johnson, my grandmother. She lived about two hours away from where my family was living at the time. I was not able to enroll for football due to living in one county and moving to another county so far away. There were many sacrifices that I had to make while living with her. We didn't have electric heaters, so I had to make a fire in the fireplace for my grandmother each morning. I would go to school smelling like smoke but it was common because many of the houses around us didn't have electric heaters. I was so glad when my uncle and aunt helped us get gas heaters to heat the house. It's a big difference when you can turn a knob and feel heat. I had to chop wood and build a fire, and go outside when it was freezing to get the wood. I can never stop thinking how that floor would feel when my feet would touch it.

My coach was George Cochran at the time, when I was in my second year of my four-year high school term. I used to work for him on his ranch with my teammate Roosevelt Peterson. My coach told me that I couldn't play football that year. I asked him if I could practice with the team, he looked at me as if he had seen a ghost. He said you must understand that you can't play, as it would be a violation against the school rules. I became the water boy for the team that year and, I told my coach that my junior year we will win the state championship. I practiced everyday with the team throughout my sophomore year and was the water boy during the games.

In my junior year, on December 8th, 1981, a year later we won the state championship. I have always tried to be a positive person in my life.

When you think positive you feel that you've become a positive person that people want to surround themselves with.

When I read about famous people like Michael Jordan and Oprah Winfrey, it brought a smile to my face. I think they are great examples of hard working, dedicated and happy individuals. When you find people that are happy, it has a way of making you feel good. When I play my son the Space Jam Movie, for a moment I feel like Michael Jordan, but when I try to slam the basketball it let's me know that I am not. When I get my microphone and talk on the air as if I have someone on my show it's all fun. I hope one day I can do what Oprah and Michael did; they reached out to people/TV viewers and made them happy. They do it without looking for anything in return and to me that is something that you have or you don't.

I never let my mind think negative when I have a seizure. My desire is to let others know that you can be successful if you stay positive. My high school coach Wayne Keahey once told me to enjoy my high school days because they are the best days of my life. I always wanted to play college football for Auburn Tigers or Alabama Crimson Tide, but unfortunately I got hurt. I can say that Philip Baker, Jimmy Burson, Jimmy Jones and Wayne Keahey wouldn't let me think negative.

They put up a sign and a quote by the Great Vincent Lombardi, it said winning is everything and that you don't do things right sometimes, you do them right all the time. I have tried to model myself after that and keep a smile on my face. I am so grateful for the people who have paved the way for me to see that you can be whatever you set your mind to be. The words that I speak are who I've become, so I say things that give hope and life to everyone.

I will keep a positive attitude and surround myself with people who think like I do. I don't want to be a part of negative thoughts, actions, interactions, and people who find them a part of that. If I do that, then this is the part of me that I don't know, so I need to know who I am at all times.

THE DANGER I FACE EVERYDAY

I live a normal life just like everyone else. My condition scares me at times because I know how severe it can be. When it causes an accident or someone has a bad fall it can cause death. How can you avoid that, as there is no way...

One day I was getting ready to go to work and had a seizure. I fell about two stories below and knocked out three of my front teeth. I was so embarrassed and didn't want to go to work and let my co-workers see me like that. I know and you know, without your smile it's hard to talk to anyone. I had to go to the dentist and get a partial made for my upper mouth, so that I would look normal again.

I had to take some time off from work because I came back the same day after having surgery. The dentist gave me about eight or night stitches in my mouth. I was trying to work but my face swelled up to about the size of a golf ball. I had to go home and use my vacation time that I didn't want to use but what could I do. I never get a chance to take a real vacation, and the reason is because something always happens and my time gets used up.

When I am driving my car I try to stay focused on what I am doing at all times. I feel I'm in a no win, win situation because if I ever have an accident due to a seizure, I know there goes my license. This is one danger that I face and I know people who drive with epilepsy will always face this negative prospect.

When you try to be the best in everything you do, an attack can set you back. It depends on how bad it is and how long it takes for your body to adjust back. I can't speak for everyone that has seizures, but I can speak for myself. I get the forewarning and/or premonition before my seizures take place. I know that something is going to happen and for a few seconds I am able to think before I lose consciousness. I can sometime hear people talking in the beginning but after that I don't know what has happened.

The feeling for me is like dizziness followed by a funny feeling that I can't describe. I am blessed to get this type of symptom. I think that it would be different if the attack comes on without a warning, that it is coming. When this happens more than one or two times I am more aware. This sometimes gives me a chance to do something or prevent me from hurting myself. I right away look for a place where I can lie down without trying to disturb others.

I will never let my dreams go. My faith in God has helped me cross over many bridges without falling in the water. I know that I will keep having seizures until a cure is found. When I look at my situation and what I am faced with, all I can do is be strong. I can only try to help develop and coach others as my day to day continues to show progress. I write down what people tell me what happens to me when they see me having a seizure. I also get a chance to see what they know.

If I had a workshop it would be called HOPE, meaning, help other people with epilepsy. The seminar would focus on finding a cure and how do we give back to the community with what we have. They would learn how to apply their talents, skills and the tools to work at getting better everyday.

I try to eat healthy and train my mind and body to think that way. I've learned that changing the crowd I used to hang out with has made my life less stressful. The company that I keep is the people who love me and understand my condition. I speak to everyone with total confidence because I've become what I believe.

We all have options in life; my choice is to treat people with love and respect. I would be lost so many times if I would have had a poor attitude. I am a winner because I choose not to be a loser. I work hard everyday on trying to reach my goals. The bible teaches us that an idle mind is the devil's workshop. I know that I am a project that will never be complete and challenges will always come my way.

Life is what you make of it. The danger I face everyday is not a mirror, I look into it only when it happens. I do have some say so in my future and that is the time when I don't have a seizure.

WHAT IS EPILEPSY?

Epilepsy is a neurological disorder that produces sudden, intense bursts of electrical activity in the brain. This abnormal electrical activity in the brain causes seizures, which may briefly upset a person's muscle control, movement, speech, vision, or awareness.

If epilepsy is not treated, seizures may occur throughout a person's life in some cases, becoming more severe and more frequent over time.

People with epilepsy have repeated seizures that usually occur without warning and often for no clear reason. My father would have repeated seizures and we never knew when they would occur.

Treatment most often involves medication. There are combinations of approaches that may be tried when medication alone does not control a person's seizures. A special diet called (ketogenic diet), a nerve stimulation device (vagus nerve stimulator), and surgery are the other options in treating epilepsy.

Epilepsy can develop at any age but it most often begins in childhood or after the age of 60. Epilepsy is sometimes the result of another condition; many cases have no known causes. Epilepsy is a long-term, on going (chronic) disorder that causes repeated seizures if it is not treated. Not everyone who has a seizure has epilepsy. Sometimes seizures occur as a result of injury, illness, or another medical condition that is not related to epilepsy. In these cases, the person does not have any more seizures once the condition improves or goes away. This is not epilepsy.

Epilepsy is not a form of mental retardation or mental illness. Seizures may look scary or strange, but they do not make a person crazy, violent, or dangerous. Children and adults may face discrimination in their school, place of work, and social lives because of others' fears and misconceptions about epilepsy. Adults with epilepsy may find their career choices limited because they cannot do certain kinds of work.

Epilepsy comes from the Greek word that means to seize, posses, attack, grab or hold. Epilepsy is not a disease. Some people with epilepsy choose not to drink at all. A seizure is most likely to happen in the morning, during the hangover process, and this is when the seizure threshold is low.

QUESTIONS ABOUT EPILEPSY

Is epilepsy hereditary?

At an early age, I saw my first cousin on my mother's side of the family having a seizure. My father had epilepsy, as did I. Also, both of my father's parents were diagnosed with epilepsy. For a long time, I believed that all epilepsy was inherited. But now, after gaining more knowledge about the disorder, I've learned that there are many causes, and that there is only a 10% chance that a child will inherit some type of epilepsy. If both parents are diagnosed with epilepsy, the chances are ten out of one hundred that their children will inherit epilepsy. If one parent has epilepsy, the chances are six out of one hundred that their children will inherit epilepsy.

If a mother has epilepsy because she has a low seizure threshold, a child of hers may inherit that low seizure threshold. If the child's father has a high seizure threshold, the child, having inherited from both parents, may not have a seizure threshold low enough to cause him or her to develop epilepsy. It is also possible that a child may inherit a genetic disease but rare a symptom of which may be epilepsy. The answer to the question I would say is "no", after learning more about it.

Can a person with epilepsy drink Alcohol?

If alcohol is taken in moderation this should not cause a problem. There is an interaction with anti-epileptic medication and alcohol.

What causes epilepsy?

Head injuries 5.5%, brain tumors 4.1%, strokes 10.9%, substance abuse 3.5% and illnesses that cause infections in the brain: 2.5%, are known causes. Epilepsy has many causes but 70% is unknown. I was born with a birthmark on my skin, and some people are born with a mark on their brain, and this may cause them to have seizures. I was dropped on my head when I was born.

Are people with epilepsy retarded?

Some people who are retarded also have epilepsy, just as some people who are retarded have other chronic illnesses. Epilepsy is not a learning disorder or a mental illness, it is a medical condition of the brain.

Should I call an ambulance if someone has a seizure?

Do not call an ambulance for a seizure unless the person does not start breathing after the seizure. This used to happen to me all the time, as it can be very expensive in the long run. If the person has one seizure right after another or injures them during the seizure, that is the time to call, if not, it is not necessary to call.

Can a person with epilepsy play sports?

If epileptic-prone patients have their seizures under control, then they can participate in sports. But always check with your doctor because sports like football and boxing are where head injuries are common, and I wouldn't recommend it.

Is epilepsy a curse?

The truth is that epilepsy is a medical disorder, and it is not a curse. Epilepsy can have both behavioral and physical symptoms because it affects the brain.

Can epilepsy be fatal?

It can happen if a seizure last more than an hour; my father kept having them one after another and lost total consciousness. It is rare that a person dies from having a seizure. A person could crash while riding a motorcycle or drown while swimming, from an epileptic seizure.

Is there a cure for epilepsy?

Medication can help control seizures in most people, but there is no cure for epilepsy.

What triggers someone with photosensitive epilepsy?

The condition is most common in adolescents, and children too can have seizures with and without flickering or flashing lights. The (EEG) electroencephalogram is one common test used to diagnose epilepsy, if there is any abnormal change in the brainwaves, photosensitive epilepsy may be diagnosed, as this will be recorded on the (EEG).

Stroboscopic lights, Sunlight coming through a line of trees, Sunlight flickering on water, Watching television, particularly if it is faulty, thereby causing a slow flicker, or if it is not tuned in properly, looking out of a window in a fast-moving airplane or train, playing video games and using other computer graphics are some of the most common triggers.

What happens when I miss a dose?

I have missed my dose in the past, and at times I can't tell if I had taken it or not. I don't think missing one dose will result in a person having a seizure. The first time I had a problem was when I took a double dose trying to make up for the time I had missed it. My doctor told me to never take both doses at the same time, and believe me, you can have a seizure. I know there is a certain amount of medication in my blood level, so I know it is important to reliably take the medication prescribed. A drug wallet can be used to help you, and will avoid confusion and prevent you from taking too many pills by mistake.

Can a person not tell their employer that they have epilepsy?

I don't think this would be something wise to do; you should let your employer know. I know there is a blank space on the employment application that asks if you have epilepsy or not. I would check the box and put, "can we discuss this part of the application". The employer needs to know due to the Health and Safety Work Act. They need to know because there are some jobs that may put your life in danger if you're not seizure free. I would say, sell yourself in your interview, and in the end let them know if your seizures are controllable or not, and provide any information that your doctor is willing to give towards your employment to work.

The Educated Patient Can Provide Support

My father passed away on May 7th, 1996. His death made me realize that there were things I needed to know about epilepsy in order to be well informed, so that I could share information about epilepsy to support family members, friends and my co-workers.

I didn't go looking for this illness; it found me when I was diagnosed with absence seizures (petit mal) at the age of eight, and by living with my father who was diagnosed with Generalized Tonic Clonic (grand mal) seizures. I experienced a lot of emotions in my childhood, as a teen, and as an adult about living with epilepsy, seeing it, and being diagnosed with it.

I know now that I was afraid because I didn't know what to do. If a person is taught the correct procedures for handling a person who is experiencing a seizure, the better he or she will feel. If I had to relive my past experiences with epilepsy over again, I would feel so much better, armed with the knowledge I now have.

I have spent many hours researching information at the public library, on the internet, and asking questions to physicians. I can now support my family, friends and co-workers with the understanding of what to do if they are faced with a person having a seizure, as I was 23 years ago.

The more I find out about this medical condition, the more I want to know. When I hear doctors talking about epilepsy, it is good to hear because I understand and can relate to what they are talking about.

The public library has been my best friend. I didn't have an email address and didn't know how to get one, so they gave me a class and signed me up for a free email account through Yahoo.com. I was computer shy but I wanted to know, so I had to apply myself to learn how to login to the Internet.

I will continue to work at the library and meet people, and help share with them what I know. I can't believe how far I have come over the years from my childhood days until now as an adult.

EPILEPSY IN THE WORKPLACE

When I began working at Chase Manhattan Bank, I didn't tell my trainer that I had epilepsy. I was afraid that I would lose my job because I was fired from my first job being out of work too much and sleeping on the job. I often had wondered if I would find an employer who would understand my condition and know what to do if I suffered a seizure on the job.

An employee shouldn't be treated differently because he or she has epilepsy. The only differences are that one person has epilepsy and the other doesn't. Studies show workers with epilepsy produce just as much work, if not more, than workers who aren't affected by epilepsy.

I think handouts for this medical condition and others should be available to employees. This may solve some of the misunderstandings about epilepsy, in addition to informing people about what to do if an epileptic incident occurs in the workplace.

I now make it my duty to tell my co-workers what to do if they witness me having a seizure. The more a person knows about epilepsy, the less frightening it will be to them.

I have been able to hold seminars through some of the health services programs to help educate people about seizures. I get a chance to hear what the outside audience has to say, and give them feedback on their questions. I let them know that epilepsy and seizures that go hand in hand with each other, are the same. The joy I get from knowing that they can take something back and share with others is a great feeling.

Epilepsy should be talked about more on TV shows; I don't see many talk show hosts tackling this subject. I know when they do, the whole world needs to be watching because it can help so many people... My dream is to one day have my own talk show, so that I can reach millions and millions of people living with epileptic seizures, and discuss different topics about epilepsy.

Can People with epilepsy live normal lives?

Yes, people with epilepsy can and do live normal lives. I am a senior collector at Chase Manhattan Bank in Tampa, Florida, where I have been employed for the past four years. I have received 15-service star awards; in 1997, I received five in that one year alone.

I volunteered in the after-school program at the Interbay YMCA, where I was a head football coach for boys aged seven to nine. We won the championship my first year as a coach and it was a great experience for the team and myself. I also served on the YMCA's annual giving campaign committee. We were responsible for raising money to donate to the various campaigns that made kids lives easier in the after school programs.

I have participated in the Great American Teach-In for the past four years. I have also tutored in the School District of Hillsborough County's reading program at Pearson Elementary School. In 1995, I donated a $500 check to this program that was presented to me by the Sallie Mae Organization, which had named me Community Service Man of the Year.

I do everything that everyone else does in life. I go bowling and fishing, as they are the things that I like to do the most. I play basketball with my friends and work out at the gym. I am like the average person with the same ability as everyone else. I try to be involved in the community as much as I can, as I believe when I meet people I've something to tell them.

The normal life I live is an inspiration to me and is educational for others. I get excited about all the things that I can do. I don't believe there is nothing I can't do. I like going into the classroom to help teach kids how to read or get them up to speed in reading.

I will never sit and let the world pass me by. I want to be able to clap my hands not because I am a hero, but because I believe in life someone has to stand in line while the heroes go by. I live my life to serve people and to deliver a performance that leaves everyone speechless.

Can a person with epilepsy drive?

Your state's Division of Motor Vehicles makes that decision based on information that is given to it from the medical department. California, Delaware, Nevada, New Jersey, Oregon and Pennsylvania are among the states that have express mandatory physician reporting requirements. Most states allow people with epilepsy to drive once they have been free of seizures for one year.

I have had a driver's license for 19 years, and have not had one accident due to epilepsy. However, always check with your doctor to make sure your seizures are under control before you drive. The patient must be truthful when applying for a driver's license or renewal; he or she must provide any medical updates that the driver's state requires.

I stopped driving for one year not because I didn't have a car, I just didn't feel comfortable even though my seizures were under control. It was fun riding the bus for a year. I got a chance to educate people on the bus about seizures, and I would pass out pamphlets that I would get from the Epilepsy Foundation of Florida.

I did a survey for one year and asked 62 respondents what would they do if they saw a person having a seizure. The number one answer for 57 of those people was, they'd put a spoon in the individual's mouth. I was glad to be able to provide the correct answer to them because I had learned it from the pamphlets that were given to me.

I missed one day from riding the bus, and that day a rider happened to have a seizure. The bus driver was so excited to see me the next day. He said that everyone was calm and they all wanted to help the person having the seizure. The friends I made on that bus will never be the same, because they all know what I know and that makes the world a better place to live in. I am glad that I wasn't there, on that day, as I would have jumped up and helped that person out, so I wouldn't have gotten a chance to see what the other bus riders had learned.

Three Common Types of Seizures

Absence, Generalized Tonic Clonic and Complex Partial are three common types of seizures.

Absence (Petit mal) is French for "small ailment." Absence seizures usually last less than 15 seconds. They may occur frequently throughout the day if untreated. Children who experience them may stop whatever they are doing and stare blankly, as they become unresponsive to their surroundings. Children may have as many as 50 or more absence seizures a day prior to being treated by medication. Most children outgrow these seizures before they reach adulthood.

Generalized Tonic Clonic (Grand mal) is French for "great ailment." Convulsions and a loss of consciousness characterize this type of epilepsy. A grand mal seizure is often called a generalized seizure; it affects the whole brain. A shortness of breath, a loss of consciousness and convulsions that can cause a person to foam at the mouth or bite their tongue are some of the signs of someone having a Generalized

Tonic Clonic (grand mal) seizure. My father and I both were diagnosed with this type of seizure.

Complex Partial is also called psychomotor or Temporal Lobe epilepsy. It is the most common seizure experienced by adults with epilepsy. These seizures usually start with a blank stare, followed by chewing, and then followed by random activity. A person appears unaware of their surroundings, may seem dazed and mumble their words. You may see a person pick at clothing, pick up objects, and try to take their clothes off. Their consciousness is impaired, and you will find that they seem afraid. You may think a person with a complex partial seizure is drunk, high, or even mentally ill.

During olden times many men and women were killed because they were believed to be possessed by demons, meaning something took control of their mind. When they described epilepsy during those times, it was called the falling sickness, as this is the kind of seizure I believe they were having.

How to handle a Grand Mal Seizure

Try to remove any object out of the person's way that may be harmful to the individual during the seizure (sharp objects, etc.). Turn the person on his or her side so that the airway is clear. Do not put anything that is tight around the neck. If they wear eyeglasses, remove them from their face. Don't try to stop or restrain the person from having the seizure. Place something soft under the person's head, or cup your hand.

Don't put anything in the person's mouth.

Don't try to give the person his or her medication during the seizure. Don't try to restrain the person during the seizure. Don't try to help the person come out of the seizure.

Do move any type of object that can hurt a person out of the way. Do keep in mind that a person feels nothing during the seizure. Do loosen anything that is tight around the person's neck.

Do turn the person on his or her side to keep a good airflow.

How to Handle a Complex Partial Seizure

Speak calmly and reassuringly to the person. Stay with the person until they're completely aware of their environment. Guide gently away from obvious hazards. Don't try to restrain. Don't grab hold unless sudden danger threatens. Don't expect verbal instructions to be obeyed.

DAY BY DAY LIVING WITH EPILEPSY

Facts About Epilepsy

Epilepsy is not like a cold; it is not contagious. Head injuries, strokes, brain tumors, substance abuse and infections of the brain are some of the known causes of epilepsy. Nothing should be placed in the person's mouth when they are having a seizure. There is no known cure for epilepsy, although there are more than 20 medications for its treatment, like Dilantin, which is the medicine I take.

Epilepsy and seizures affect 2.3 million Americans of all ages and about 50 million people worldwide.

An estimated 316,000 children aged 14 and under have epilepsy, so do 1.4 million adults under the age of 64, and 550,000 aged 65 and over.

10% of the American population will experience a seizure in their lifetime, and 3% will develop epilepsy by age 75.

Approximately 181,000 new cases of seizures and epilepsy occur each year. In 1995, the annual financial cost of epilepsy in the United States was $12.5 billion dollars.

Patients With Epilepsy

Try to have a set time you take your medication each day. Try not to miss your dosage and ask your doctor what to do if you do miss a dosage.

Never stop taking your medication because you feel okay; follow your doctor's directions.

Parents of children with epilepsy should ask your child's neurologist about the ketogenic diet.

Alcohol consumption can decrease the effectiveness of your medication and may induce a seizure.

Wear a helmet when riding a bicycle, skating or engaging in other rigorous physical activities.

Keep a list of your current medications in case you need to inform others such as hospital personnel and emergency medical technicians.

Remember to have someone write down a description of what they see when you are having a seizure.

Purchase a medic-alert bracelet with epilepsy written on it.

LIVING WITH EPILEPSY

When my friends first saw me having a seizure, their reaction was what I had expected. They were afraid and didn't want to be around me because they didn't know what to do. In the 80's we were told that a person could swallow their tongue and choke to death.

It is impossible for someone to swallow his or her tongue. They confused mental illness and special education programs with seizures because of the strange behavior that a seizure can produce. I haven't seen my high school girlfriend and most of my friends since we graduated. This book is my way of educating them as well, and myself of the myths and misconceptions that we had back then. I hope one day I get the chance to see her and my old friends again, so I can let them know that I'm doing fine in life.

When an individual works for a company, they have to remember it's not the company that makes life good or bad for you. What I mean is, a company like Wendy's is always going to be there. I have walked away many times due to management because I'm too soft with people, and I always think about the struggle I have with epilepsy. The company will be there for me, so if management is good then people don't have to walk away. In my first job I was fired not due to management, but trying to understand my medication and the way it works for me. Dilantin is a medication that I use to treat my seizures.

Moreover, my son is doing fine now, he has not had a seizure in over two years. He can play sports and do what most other kids can do. I think he will grow out of having seizures and live a normal life just like the other kids. In the house I teach him small things like, don't turn on the oven, use the microwave, we never use glass containers, only plastic. He can't take a bath unless there is an adult in the house. I don't let him fill up the tub with water; I feel a shallow bath is safer. He is a great kid, and I know his life will go on as well as mine.

I try very hard to keep a positive attitude, but some things you just can't control. Life is not like a faucet where you can turn it on and off. I can drink hot water or cold water if I want to because I have the power in my hand to do that, and I can make it sweet or bitter.

When you deal with epilepsy, each day is a day. You don't know what to expect and you don't know how it's going to be. I try to remain focused on what life has in store for me that day. I try to avoid being overtired and being bored because this is the time that I can have a seizure. I had to quit college due to having a seizure, and find it hard at times to mix with people. Frustration sometimes builds up inside of me and dealing with that can be a problem to manage for me.

I wish I had all the answers to every question that a person wants to ask. Epilepsy to me reminds me of a battery in a car. It has a positive and a negative... Have you ever had to give someone a jumpstart, to start their car's engine. When you think about it everything has to be right, the red has to go with the positive, and the black has to go with the negative. The connection has to be the same and they have to understand that everything must fire correctly at the same time. When they misfire or someone makes the mistake and crosses the positive and negative wires together, the engine goes into a brainstorm and that's how I think the brain reacts sometimes; it doesn't know what to do. I have done that to my friend's car and the sparks that fly out from that battery is shocking. I can't imagine having the job of a brain, as I wouldn't know where to begin and where to end.

I hope one day that I can write a second book on my life story. I would call it The Ralph Brook's Story and get Denzel Washington to play me, and that would be something. A book and a movie with my favorite actor playing me, what else could I ask for. I'm holding on to all of my dreams if Mr. Washington can do it, I know I can.

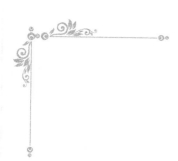
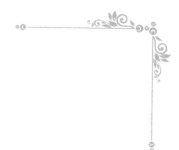

Poetry and Children's Poem CPPGS80-91

Ralph Brooks Poetic Reflections

Day By Day

In my life things tend to come and go,
But why they do,
I may never know.
I've learned to live with the bad
As well as the good
Because I know
Things do not always work the way they should.
In my life when things go wrong
I ask myself "Am I weak
Or am I strong?"
If I am weak
I hold my head up high,
And look for the stars in the sky.
If I am strong
I can go on,
Because what is going to be,
Will be.
I take one day at a time
Trying to be content,
Knowing it can control my mind and hoping in the end that I am fine.
When my day seems to be so bad
I just close my eyes,
And wish for things I could have had.
Life itself has so much to give,
So day by day
I choose the way I live.

My Talk To My Son

On August 7, 1997 my son cried out loud,
Seeing you come into this world, made me feel proud. There was never a doubt or a maybe,
I knew you were my baby.
When I first saw your smile,
I was so glad that you were my child.
Before you came into my life, I would sit and ponder, Of how life makes you wonder.
If life is worth living,
When all you seem to do is to be giving.
Half the time, in my mind, I felt like I was losing, Because everything was so confusing.
Just when I had put everything aside,
You came along and gave me back my pride.
It was not so much your smile that made me glad, But the thought that one day,
You'd be calling me dad.
No longer do I sit and ponder,
If my life is going under.
You make my life worth living,
And you make my life worth giving.
You're daddy's little man, so while you're maturing,
I will work on a future plan.
I will give you my all, and will pick you up whenever you fall.
So when I am old and gray, and can't pick up my footstep, My son, I will look for your help.
Because there is one thing, I can say,
In my heart you will always stay.

Kids Stay In School

A promise to stay in school is the golden rule,
Because some kids will struggle with school.
Parents should make themselves this promise,
A promise to keep them in school
Is their golden rule.
To always be there for their kids,
To teach them just like their parents did.
Most kids want to do things without their parents,
But a parent should always stay involved.
Parents have to stop it before it starts,
And the welfare of a kid starts with you.
When parents walk through the mall,
They see kids big and small.
It brings a smile to his or her face.
But when the kid talks back to his mother,
The smile leaves your face,
For a kid to bring shame to his mother,
Is a disgrace.
Your mother brought you into this world,
She could have wanted a boy,
But instead she got a girl.
The mother's outlook doesn't change.
You will be treated the same,
The mother just has to change the baby's name.

Kids, everyday should be like its January first,
You don't have to wait 'til the beginning of the year,
To make a New Year's resolution,
To stay in school every day should be the solution.
Parents, there are no guarantees in life
That your kid won't quit school;
Some kids will act as a fool.
But you as a parent,
You have a golden rule,
And that is trying to keep your kid in school.

Always Give God The Glory

You have to keep your eyes on the prize,
When there is a job to do,
You should never worry about the size.
The most important thing is that God is with you.
When you give God the glory,
You can be like David and Goliath in history.
David was a little shepherd boy,
Whom God knew had a great love for his sheep,
The kind of love that nothing could destroy.
A bear and a lion one day
Tried to show him his grave,
He killed them both and remained brave.
Goliath was a giant in size,
He took his eyes off the prize.
The Philistines feared him more than God.
When Goliath went against God,
He looked at David and laughed.
He said, "You are so small,
I am Goliath and I am almost ten feet tall."
Goliath said, "My power is in my spear,
You Israelites better never come near."
David said, "My power is in the God of Abraham;
My god is why I am.
When a bear and a lion came looking for a meal,
My God met me in the field."
David took a stone and hit Goliath in the head.
The Israelites rejoiced because the giant had fallen dead.
Whatever you do in life, always put God first
And always give God the glory,
Your life will be a forever-reading story

American Poet

I have always wanted to write poetry
That people all over the world would be able to read.
As hard as it may seem,
One day I will fulfill my dream.
One day,
I will walk into a bookstore
And as I read the display on the floor,
The sign will say,
"Soon to come, Ralph Brooks,
Book of Poetry: What Can I Say About It?"
I will wait for that day.
As a writer I have always been true from the start,
My words have always come from the heart.
There is one lesson every writer must learn,
To have your book put on a shelf,
Does not mean that respect is earned.
That is something a teacher can't teach,
And a preacher can't preach.
You have to search yourself day by day,
Because honesty is the only way.
In my poems I always have a meaning,
An understanding from beginning to end.

I don't write poems just to make up rhymes
Or to find words that sound good,
Or waste my readers' time.
It would be like living in my own dream
And traveling from place to place
Without any means.
I know that this road can be long
But I won't stop until it is well known.
Whether or not you know it,
I am an American poet.

Change

People say you and I don't belong,
I have to ask myself,
How can something that feels so right
Seem so wrong?
When we would walk down the street,
People would look at us strange,
Like saying, "Keep your distance,"
And don't come within their range.
What happened to?
"All people are treated the same."
The person who made that statement,
Is this the person whom I should blame?
I'm not an expert on what words to use,
But to say all people are treated the same,
This is the one phrase that I will not use.
We live in this country,
Where people are of different races,
And we see so many different faces.
So quickly we begin to judge,
And for no reason,
Our fellowman, we hold a grudge.
We as people must be willing to change,
To change for the better,

So that we live not in fear with one another.
In my own country,
I feel that I am the tourist,
And my life is always at risk.
It is sad to say, but it is true.
Don't ask society if we belong,
There is and old saying,
"Can we all just get along?"

A Cloud Of Endless Rain

Here I sit
In a world of pain,
Lost in a cloud of endless rain.
Since you left,
I realized,
You only cared about yourself.
You made me feel very small,
Two weeks,
You have been gone.
At least,
I should have received a phone call.
Now I sit watching time
Because you are no longer mine.
My feelings are not the same.
No longer
Do my tears feel like rain?
The last time
You looked into my eyes,
I am not the same guy,
Who found it hard to say good-bye?
So I say to you my dear,
Your words I do not hear.
You say

You've changed now.
My question to you is, how?
I always gave you a second chance,
But this time,
Your ways
No longer hold me in a trance.
Now it is my time to watch you;
I can see you are feeling the pain,
But I am blind by your cloud of endless rain.

Not What I Do Most

This note is not to make you sad.
I just express my thoughts better
With pen and pad.
So whenever you decide to come home,
You will realize that I am gone.
There will be a note on your dresser
Saying, "I can no longer handle your pressure."
You can act like you just don't know
What I am talking about,
But let me refresh your mind,
So there is no shadow of a doubt.
I was your faithful boyfriend,
But when we would leave home,
You would tell everyone I was just a friend.
Then you would look at me,
You would give me a smile and a little poke,
Knowing that my spirit was broken.
You make me feel like a puppet on a string,
While you roam around doing
Almost anything and everything.
What we had is gone.
What I have to do is move on.

So before you throw this note away,
Listen to what I have to say.
Just try being a good apple,
An apple of good taste.
You don't have to pretend to be my girlfriend,
If you are only just a friend.
Then there is no trace of a doubt,
What this relationship is all about.
This note has to come to an end,
For the first time as I look up at my bedpost,
Missing you is not what I do most.

Can We Chat?

The very first sight of you,
My heart burst into flames.
A part of me
Wanted to chat.
The other part
Was not cool with that.
You sat there,
All poised and sweet,
While my heart skipped a beat.
I kept trying
To make eye to eye contact,
But I just couldn't find the right act.
I know to point at someone
Is not nice.
I had to do something
To break the ice.
I wanted to ask you your name,
But my nerves I couldn't tame.
I was still in a daze,
As smoke filled the place
Like a morning haze.
"Last round," the bartender shouts,
I knew my time was running out.

My friends continued to talk more and more
As you made your way to the door.
Still trying to make eye contact,
I just couldn't find the right act.
The feeling of sweat in my palms.
The feeling of excitement,
And trying to remain calm.
At first,
A part of you was not all right with that,
Nice to see both parties want to chat.

True Friendship

When I think of a true friendship,
I think
Of a brother and sister relationship.
A true friendship
Is a friend who means a lot.
A friend
Will always care no matter what you got.
A friend will always help you,
When no one else will,
Like thrusting money into your pocket,
To pay the phone bill.
A friend,
Is someone who picks up the slack
And will always give you a pat on the back.
A true friend,
You can never measure,
When they do things for you,
They gladly say,
"My pleasure."
On the days you are feeling blue,

A friend
Will always be there;
For a friend that's nothing new.
A true friendship is all about good;
A friend will do what no other would.
When you are down,
A friend
Will always be around.
A true friendship
Is a special kind of ship.
When I think of a true friendship, I think
Of a brother and sister relationship.

Who Could It Be?

He won
The World Heavyweight Title in 1964.
He'd done
What no man had done before.
He was champion of the world three times. He gave
The American people so many thrills.
Like the "Thriller from Manila,"
He made
The whole world stand still.
His name was a freedom symbol.
On Olympic day,
He carried the torch,
He kept walking,
As his hand trembled.
He has always had a strong desire;
No one can put out his fire.
He made boxing fun,
And more than just a sport.
He is a true role model,
Whom the world showed a lot of support.
He has been called "The greatest of all time."
He was Sports Illustrated's 20th Century Man.
Think a little harder if you can.
He is a legend in the boxing Hall of Fame.
Cassius Clay is no longer his name.
Who could this gentleman be?
They say he floats like a butterfly,
And stings like a bee.
This man has to be Muhammad Ali.

Your Dreams Are What Make You

Dreams can come true;
Your dreams are what make you.
You may not always achieve your goal
But that doesn't mean you are a failure.
You must look deep in your soul.
Whatever you want you will find.
You have to reset your mind,
Just like a tape fast-forwards, then rewinds.
Sometimes we feel life doesn't give us
A fair chance.
Someone once said a singer is made to sing,
And a dancer is made to dance.
If your dreams are what you have inside,
There is no need for the dark to hide.
You develop a plan,
A plan to make you the best,
And your dreams will take care of the rest.
When you were in first grade,
You were taught your ABC's.
To learn them at first you couldn't see;
You felt uncomfortable in some ways.
Yet, the alphabet,
You still know from your childhood days.
When we get older in life we sometimes forget,
But like learning your ABCs,
Dreams are something that stays with you.
That's something no one can take from you.
Just be all you can be,
And your dreams will take care of you.

Love Is

Love is sure, Love is pure,
Love is something the doctor can't cure.
Love can be an inspiration,
That inspires you during a rough situation.
Love is like your first kiss,
Nerves, butterflies in your stomach.
Love can make you feel like this.
Love is so many things.
Love can be a diamond ring.
That ring can signify
The love one has in a marriage,
No matter who is pushing the baby carriage.
Love is respect
You have for one another,
Love is what holds the family together.
Love is sure, Love is pure,
Love always makes you feel secure.
Love can be hard to explain.
Love can be a feeling that you feel,
But you know that feeling is real.
Love can be a special moment
Like finding a four-leaf clover,
It's something hard to get over.
What is Love?
Love is a gift from the heavenly father up above.
Love is free.
Love is for you,
Love is for me.
Love is not something you can wrap
Or put beneath the Christmas tree. Love is for the whole world to see.

What Can I Say?

Death is a serious tragedy,
That I deal with everyday.
When it happened to my loved one,
It left me empty,
Not much I could say.
The grief was so hard to bare
At times,
I found myself gasping for air.
Despite the pain and sorrow;
How am I supposed to feel?
Understanding that my loved one
Will not be here tomorrow.
Death has no schedule;
It could happen day or night.
It doesn't ask the question, who is right?
I believe as long as I live on this earth,
There is a time to die,
And a time to give birth.
The one thing that I don't know
Is, when is it my time to go?
But I must be ready at all times,
Because only God knows.
When I will breathe my last breath,
And only God knows,
When will I face death?
Death is a serious tragedy,
That I have dealt with in my own way.
Now that it has happened to my loved one,
I understand and know what to say.

Memories

I remember
Our small talks,
I remember
Our long walks.
Late night conversation,
Building off each other's expectation.
Even though we drifted apart,
you will always be in my heart.
Memories
Can last a lifetime.
Tiny moments
Pass a day at a time.
Bound
By the thoughts of the past,
That we would always last.
You will always
Be my inspiration.
Late night conversation,
Building off each other's expectations.
In the long run
We will have fun.
I know
You had to leave town,
I know
I let you down.
You still mean
The world to me.
Many years have gone by;
I still find it hard
To deal with the memories.

Very Nice To See

A man
To open the car door,
Don't see that any more.
A man
To pull out the chair,
A man
To comb back your hair.
A man
To give you his paycheck,
And man to show love and respect.
A man
To be the man,
A man
Who understands.
A man
Who will take you out at night, A man
Who comes home before daylight.
I will do
What your man wants to do.
Let me get the door,
And drive you by bay shore.
Let me comb your hair,
While your man sits and stares.
I know your automobile
Was in a car wreck,
Go ahead and take my paycheck.
What did you say?
Very nice to see
Someone taking care of me.

Childhood

Don't know
Good or bad.
Don't know
Happy or sad.
Don't know
Calm or mild.
Don't know
If I was a kid or child.
When I was small
I wanted it all.
I didn't care,
I didn't have to pay the cost, but it was a big deal
If a penny was lost.
One thing
I always had on my mind, To have fun,
And to do it all the time.
Today
I miss being a kid.
I don't miss
Getting a spanking
For the wrong I did.
No girlfriend,
No wife,
That's the time of your life.
When I was a child
I loved to be crazy and wild. I miss those days,
Not knowing
Good or Bad,
Not knowing
Happy or Sad.

First

First,
I laid eyes on you.
Then,
I began to wonder
Is it a dream,
That to me,
You look
Sweeter than
Peaches and cream.
My everything,
Nice manicure,
Nice pedicure,
A work of art.
Beautiful and smart,
What a woman.
My life
Will never be the same.
I don't care,
If I don't know your name.
This must be
A dream,
I thought,
I heard a scream.
Who's hand is this shaking my shoulder,
Telling me to roll over.
Whose eyes do I see?
First, I was looking at them,
Now, They are looking at me.

How Long Has It Been

I know
It's been a longtime.
I hope
You've been doing fine.
How long has it been,
We both lost a good friend.
We both
Cried in the end.
I want
To reach for you,
I don't want to feel,
The way
That I do.
I left you sad,
And for that
I feel bad.
I won't waste your time,
It has been a longtime.
I want
To reach for you,
A wish among the stars.
A star that seems so far.
How long has it been?
Can I be your friend?

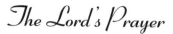
The Lord's Prayer

Our father,
Which art in heaven,
Hollowed Be thy name.
Thy Kingdom Come.
Thy will be done In earth,
As it is in heaven.
Give us this day our daily bread and
Forgive us our debts,
As we forgive our debtors.
And Lead us not
Into temptation, But
Deliver us from evil;
For thine Is the Kingdom,
And the Power,
And the Glory,
Forever.
Amen.

Meeting My Son's School Teacher

We had a meeting about my son
She explained to me,
All he had done.
He got off
To a slow start.
He understands,
He must work hard In order to be smart.
His teacher
Went on and on.
She had nothing
But good things to say.
She said
He wants to win,
And that
He has so many friends.
I wish he were there
To see how much
His teacher really cares.
What a thrill,
Hard to say
How I feel.
Can't wait to get home,
To let him know
How proud I am of him.
I know he works hard.
He got a free bowling pass
Because he had a perfect attendance card.

My Senior Year (Class of 1983)

My senior year,
It was the best,
Thank God,
I passed my ACT test.
I was the first one
In my family
To finish school.
My mother and I thought that was cool.
I had
My whole
Life ahead of me,
I was voted
Best dressed of the class.
I owe
Everything to my mother.
She kept me looking good,
Always buying me nice clothes And shoes,
And doing
More than a mother should.
Twenty years,
Have come and gone.
By the grace of God, I'm still holding on.
My senior year
Was the best,
Not because,
I passed the ACT test.

I made history,
I had done what no one else
In my family had done.
I finished high school,
And I was the first one.

A Shout Out To All The Rappers

I'm Ralph Brooks,
The ladies choice,
The coolest
Of all the homeboys.
At the age of three
I was bouncing Off my mama's knee.
At the age of four I was jamming,
Like never before.
At the age of five:
Sunday
Monday
Tuesday
Wednesday
Thursday
Friday and Saturday,
The sugar hill gang
Was keeping it live.
All the ladies
Love my style and grace.
Can't help but to watch
This handsome face.
I drive the ladies wild
With my cool walk.
They stand in line
Just to hear me talk.

I'm six feet one
Full of fun,
Cool as I want to be,
Stand on of top of the world
For all the ladies to see.
People ask how I got this way,
Simple, I grew up watching Morris Day.
Until you find It,
I wanted
To be a football star, and run
The ball far.
I wanted
To play basketball, and grow
At least 7 feet tall.
I wanted
To play baseball,
And hit
The ball over the wall.
I wanted
To ride a motorcycle,
And race
My friend Michael.
I wanted
To be an actor,
And have
My own TV show,
Or be like Oprah,
Who the world knows.

I can
Do it all
I don't have to choose one,
My life Isn't done.
What I have,
I have to use it
Or lose it.
If not,
Never mind it,
Until you find it.

A Penny On Head

Good luck, Bad luck
How long does it last;
I don't know,
But I have been told,
About
A tale of the past.
The story goes,
If you
Find a penny on head,
Pick it up,
Put it into your pocket,
And
Good luck
Will come your way.
If you
Find a penny on tails,
Pick it up,
And
Throw it away,
But
Bad luck
Will come your way.
If I find
A penny on head,
Good luck
Will come my way.

If I find
A penny on tails,
I'm going to
Flip it over to head,
Put it in my pocket,
So good luck can come my way.

The Magic In Your Eyes

My first glance
My first dance
My first chance
My first romance.
Can I say This again,
My first romance
My first chance
My first dance
My first glance.
See what I meant, is
I want
To go forward,
But
My mind is going backwards.
The magic
In your eyes,
Made me realize.
I have to wait
For my first date.
I just happened
To be in the right place,
At the right time.
In Spanish
They have a word
That means hot,

I couldn't move
From that spot,
The word I forgot.
My first glance
My first dance
My first chance,
My first romance.

Grandparents

They know
Just what to do.
They are the remedy For your kids
And you.
When the kids,
Are under the weather,
They have a way
Of making them feel better.
You sometimes
Have to make that call
When the kids,
Are driving you
Up the wall?
You just
Want a break,
No more can you take.
So you
Load the kids
In the car
And head
To the Grandparents house,
Who don't live far.
Grandparents
Are special and dear,
And
Have a way of letting you know
That they Are always near.

Cold World

Money is low
Business is slow
Don't know Which way to go.
I feel misused
I got refused
For a job Shucking Corn on the cob.
That's sad
You know.
I must be
Shooting bad.
I only make
Enough to get by.
I live
Paycheck to Paycheck.
At times,
I want to cry.
Rent is due
Here comes
The landlord Sue.
I need
To win the Lotto.
Six lucky numbers
Will be my motto.
I know,
I'm not the owner Of silver and gold,
that's why
This world is so cold.

The Barber Shop

Fade
Edge
Hair design
Get it all,
It's your call.
Your input,
The wait can be long While you sit
On your butt.
You will wait,
There is nothing
Like a fresh haircut.
People come
From all round.
You sit and watch
Hair falling down
To the ground.
Kids running
Here and there,
All you
Can do
Is stare.
You are the king
When they call your name.
That sound from the clippers
Is the sweetest thing.
The wait is over
Jump into the chair
And let the barber cut your hair.

Coffee And Tea

Coffee
Coffee
Tea
Tea
I like coffee,
I like tea,
Which one
Will it be.
May I have a cup,
Just fill it up.
Which one,
Coffee or Tea.
Can't make
My mind up,
Just pour me a cup
Of coffee and tea.
Which one
I drink,
We will have to see.
Is today
Wednesday,
The middle weekday,
The day
We call hump day.
My eyes are in a slump;
Give me
Coffee and tea
To get me over the hump.

Pour me a fresh cup.
Let me
Smell that smell.
If it's flavor
Everyone can tell.
They will finish the pot,
Nothing like Coffee and Tea, hot.

As Long As I Live

My sister
My mother
My brother
My father,
I will
Always love my family.
My niece
My nephew
My cousin
My aunt
My uncle
My grandmother
My grandfather,
I will
Always love my family.
My soul
My mind
My body
My heart,
I will
Give all I have.
My sister
My mother
My brother
My father,
As long
As I live,
As long
As my heart
Has love to give, I will Always love my family

My High School Girlfriend

I'm writing
You a letter
To let
You know,
I can calm
Any storm or weather.
If you,
For any reason,
Get sick,
Call me on my phone,
And ask for Nick.
If your car
Just happens
To break down,
And for no reason
I'm not around,
Don't you panic.
I'm a certified mechanic.
If you want
Something from the store,
And you've got no flow,
Meet me at the bay,
Where I will be stacking hay.
I'll tell my boss,
You'll be picking up my pay.
There is nothing
For you I wouldn't do.
I will give you the world,
Buy you diamonds and pearls.
You are My high school girl.

Born In Alabama

Football
Is the talk.
Eufaula, Alabama is my hometown,
People come from all around.
To fish
And hunt,
They are happy to see
The winter months.
Football
Fishing
Hunting
What more
Could you ask for.
Where these sports
Are bigger than life.
Where you see
The husband,
Usually you see
The wife.
In Alabama,
To have been born,
To pull a cow by the horn,
Is something special for me.

The place
Will always be dear,
Growing up a country boy.
I didn't always speak clear.
But,
All anyone wants to know
Is, who are you for,
Auburn Tigers or Alabama Crimson Tide?

911

God Bless America
God Bless America
God Bless America,
I kept saying that
So many times,
911
Stays on my mind.
An answer
I can't find.
Can't get right
Ever since
I've seen that site.
Crime takes
A serious bite.
I visited
New York City
Where
The night-lights
Look so pretty.
It's such a shame
The Big Apple
Will never
Be the same.
I was
Trying to have fun
Everyone
Was on the run.

The weather was so cold,
My thin suit,
The wind ran through.
New York City,
What a place to see.
New York City,
What a place to see 91, always a part of me.

Spanish Music

I love
To hear
Spanish music;
It has a sexy sound,
As smooth as
Rain falling down.
The words,
I don't understand
But I am a fan.
I listen to it,
Everyday of the week,
The salsa dance I seek.
The language
I want to speak,
So with poetry
And Spanish music
Many people
I can reach
To do poetry.
In Spanish music
I want someone
To teach.
When
I find myself in trouble,
I don't have to pour me a double. I put on my Spanish music
And it calms my troubled world.

The music,
I will never stop playing.
One day
I will understand
What the words are saying,
Until then I will follow,
While the ladies laugh and hollow.

McDonald's

My son's
Favorite place to eat.
It's No problem With getting him To sit in his seat.
Hamburger, Cheeseburger, French fries,
He points
With his eyes.
He Is
Full of joy.
He knows
The happy meal pack
Has a snack
Or a special toy.
When
It's time to go
He runs
To do the door,
And falls on the floor.
The rides he found,
And wants to go on the playground.
As he
Begins to cry
I hand him
A French fry,
A smile
Comes to his face.
A voice speaks;
My name is Ronald,
I'm glad you came to McDonald's.

Merry-Go-Round

The Merry-Go-Round
The Merry-Go-Round
The Merry-Go-Round,
It goes
Round and round.
It's like a spinning
top. No one knows
Where it will stop.
Your head
May feel a little light,
But hold on tight.
Drag your feet on the ground.
Who cares
About falling down.
The ride,
Going in circles
And more circles.
You want it to last,
You and your friends
Are having a blast.
Someone hollow more,
So someone push more.
All of a sudden
You hear this thunder,
The gray clouds
Take away the sun,
Just when,
Everyone is having fun.

No more daylight.
The Merry-Go-Round Is
closed for the night.
You and your friends
Had a blast.
You had fun
As long as the ride last.

I Love To Swing

I love to swing
I love to swing
I love to swing,
I don't care
If I get a bang.
I love to swing
I love to swing
I love to swing,
Whatever
My parents ask
To swing,
I'll do anything.
I love
To swing fast.
I love
To swing slow.
I love
To try to touch the sky,
And watch
The birds fly by.
When I swing,
I love to race.
When I swing,
I like to compete,
And win first place.

To swing
How fast,
To swing
How slow,
I don't care,
Just don't let me fall below.

Rainbow

Do you know
The reason why
There is a rainbow,
With all the different colors,
Half part of the sky.
I have an idea,
The story is old,
But I have been told.
God wanted Noah
To build
A new world,
So he could
Destroy the old world.
He gathers,
Animals, two of every kind,
Through the blowing wind.
He put them into a boat
That served as an overcoat.
To protect them from the flood,
To replace bad and evil
With good.
Forty days and Forty nights,
It rained,
No one could go outside.
Everyone had to stay inside.

The one-day,
The sun shone again,
A rainbow appeared
As a sign from God,
That he wouldn't destroy
The world by water again.

Putting Your Children To Bed

They fight sleep
Back and forth,
You go into the room to take a peep.
Nothing like a baby's scent,
You take a sniff,
And a kiss on the cheek.
It's a way of speaking,
And hope
They remain sleeping.
Oh well,
Another story to tell,
One opens,
And you take a look,
Time to read another book.
You go
To the rocking chair,
While
They eat, look and stare.
With your mouth closed,
You begin hum and rock,
Staring at the clock.
It's going to be
A long night,
You can't even dim the light.
A hush comes
When you hear noise,
Everything must be quiet;

A sudden sound
Can take away the poise.
Silence and stillness,
So you rub their head
And slowly put them into bed.
You go to your room
Knowing you have to wake up soon.

Time-Out

Kids
Don't always do
What mommy or daddy say,
Time-out,
A place
They have to go.
Good behavior
Can shorten
The time they stay.
Bad behavior
Can make
It a long day.
They have
To understand
The correct way.
As a child
They must be trained early,
So they don't run wild.
This is our task,
Help from someone else,
We shouldn't have to ask.
It hurts us
As parents.
It's like having a list
Of what to do,
And how much did we miss.

We don't
Want to move anything
To the next day,
We call time out,
And get it out of the way.

Giraffe

Boys and Girls,
Did you know
The Giraffe,
Is the tallest
Animal in the world?
Boys and Girls,
Did you know,
In the jungle
They are easily found,
Its head
Is high above the ground.
The Giraffe
Can see
A very long distance,
If danger is near,
It can move instantly.
They have long legs
And run very fast.
With their speed,
Most animals they will pass.
The Giraffe
Loves to eat leaves;
It has one advantage,
It can reach high
And get leaves from the trees.
Boys and Girls,
Now you know
The Giraffe
Is the tallest
Animal in the world.

In Day By Day Living With Epilepsy, Ralph V. Brooks narrates his life experience with epilepsy through personal essays, educational articles, children's poetry and a collection of poems. With a desire to influence and educate the general public about this medical condition, he provides information about care, treatment, safety precautions, and the difficult life decisions that face those with epilepsy.

Mr. Brooks supports people who have epilepsy by demonstrating his leadership in the workplace as well as in his community, including his ongoing involvement with youth sports activities, first as a player, now as a coach. He shows by example how a person with epilepsy can lead a normal, fulfilling, and a rewarding life. His hope is that workplaces, athletic venues, schools and other educational institutions will use this book to enlighten the public about epilepsy.

> "It is refreshing to have an individual
> talk from his heart about his life experiences."
> ---Thomas L. Orth

Thanks To Famous People With Epilepsy

Charles Dickens is known as one of the greatest English novelists of all time. He once said that to be a productive writer, one must have patience, self-discipline, and keep the mind in good working order. I've always tried to follow his advice. Dickens made people realize that writing is not as easy as people might think it is. Despite his constant struggle with epilepsy, he managed to write 16 major novels in the 1800s, and his writing still has a direct impact on readers today.

Alfred Nobel was a brilliant man who invented dynamite in 1867. He invested his money in the Russian oil fields and other small businesses, and with the fortune he amassed, he established the Nobel Prize, .

First awarded in 1901, the Nobel Prize is given in his honor, on December 10th of each year, marking the date of his death and celebrating the accomplishments of human endeavor.

Vincent van Gogh was a Dutch painter. His paintings are some of the world's most famous works of art. His story ends with tragedy; he had problems with mental illness and his seizures continued. At the age of 37 he killed himself.

Napoleon Bonaparte was one of the most brilliant military figures in history. In 1804, he declared himself the emperor of France.

Lewis Carroll is most famous for writing Through The Looking Glass and Alice's In Wonderland.

Pyotr Ilyich Tchaikovsky, and his ballet The Nutcracker is a Christmas favorite around the world. He was a Russian music composer famous for many operas, symphonies and ballets.

When I think of the works of these six gentlemen, who lived with epilepsy and whose lives have inspired me to be all that I can be; I believe all things are possible to people who have epilepsy, if they believe in themselves.

CPSIA information can be obtained
at www.ICGtesting.com
Printed in the USA
LVHW090902210820
663747LV00001B/114